to Arlie

iii

CONTENTS

I. FAR

II. NEAR

NEAR AND FAR

AL ZOLYNAS

GARDEN OAK PRESS

I

FAR

Near and Far

for BOB INGRAHAM

He set the smartphone's alarm
for just before midnight
to catch the full lunar eclipse,
the rare blood moon,
and out of a dream of running through mountains
he awoke to the sound of
the Stones' *Satisfaction*,
which they still can't get no.
Disoriented, confused,
he fumbled at the little device in the dark,
pressing at its smooth surfaces.

Something flashed around his fingers,
white light and a phosphene reaction on his retina
like mini comets and meteors.
He rolled out of bed, woke his wife, opened
the door to the deck, and they looked up and up
to the moon directly above
just to the side of pine branches, small
with a little bite out of it like a cartoon cookie and
just turning orange. And that was that,
the little midnight celebration of a rare
astronomical event, not too dramatic, but lovely
in the way of these things, making
us feel for a moment part
of the bigger picture.

In the morning,
when he opened up his smartphone,
a strange small picture appeared, something
purple and red and intensely white
at the center, all against a black background.
It looked like a photograph sent back
from the Hubble Space Telescope, some distant
nebula, eons of light years away.
Where did it come from, this bizarre and gorgeous
picture of distant space?

Then he recalled last night's flash of light,
deduced the accidental firing of the phone's camera,
his own fingers captured in that midnight moment,
translucent, glowing red and white hot,
the Great Three-Fingered Nebula
of near and far.

Why Old Men Watch Old Movies

Not for the intricate plots they no longer follow
the dramatic payoff, resolve

maybe for Yul Bryner
his enviable abundance of testosterone

movie snow, too, of course
its beautiful cold-free falling

places they've been or not
the Mediterranean just for a glimpse

of Odysseus lashed to the mast
(oh, how they know that feeling)

a slower pace, the soundtrack they
hear shuffling from room to room

yesterday's funky and familiar equipment
blue-metaled six-guns, rotary phones

cars whose only sound system's the thud of
slammed door, the roar of an eight unwinding

oh, and, of course, those Tyrolean hats with perky brushes
like the ones they affected in their youth

An Egg from the Eclipse

Our chickens really did file back
into the shed and settle down
in the darkness
that flowed over us at noon.
Ten minutes later,
the rooster emerged —
unrested, confused —
and crowed in a cracked voice,
and the interrupted day continued
brighter than before.
And later,
just before the standard sunset,
my mother asked me to check
for eggs again, and there really
was one, thin-shelled,
malformed
lying in its nest
of shredded newspaper.
I carried it into the house
and we all marveled, passing
it around carefully,
an egg from the eclipse.

Incubation

Caught Jupiter, that old benefic,
and his moons
on the Today Show this morning —
Ganymede, Io, Callisto, Europa — untold miles away
in my dining room
while I ate a waffle and yogurt before work.

There they are again, full color
on the front page
looking like someone's notion
of abstract pizza
(for all that scientists can tell us,
something out there, after all,
made of cheese).

Outside, it's early spring in Southern California,
the third day of a Santa Ana
after much rain and flooding:
three days blazing up in a glory
of new beginnings.
Who's to say this isn't the first Wednesday
of the first week of creation?

I get into my old VW
with its 175,000-mile odometer
(this morning the distance from Voyager One to Jupiter)
and drive off through the weird suburban
universe into the flow of the freeway

under an impossibly blue sky.

In the parking lot,
I step out of my car for the first time —
like the first robin of spring
stepping out of the shells
of the only life it's never known.

The Only Tree

When the only tree
in our back yard started to dry out,
I, a boy of ten, thought of the changes
of seasons, how nature cycles through, how
what leaves always returns . . .
but, just in case any help was needed,
I watered the tree with the hose every day after school,
watered it around the trunk, on the trunk,
                                    up along the spread
branches, among the long leaves, turning silver-grey
in the slant of afternoon sun,
and when I climbed into it
with my snack of cookies,
I think I talked to it with my cells:
Tree, you'll be OK; don't die . . . .

And when the last leaf fell and it was clear
the tree was dead,
I don't think I was ever sadder.
What was that ten-year-old's grief,
unmatched, though since surpassed
by all that adults endure or are broken by?
The mystery of that young heartache
is still with me, its unspeakable keenness
and purity. I knew not
to share it with anyone and I learned how
to carry it and even bury it
close to the roots, the tips
where failure falls back on itself
and something new begins to grow.

Bread, in Gratitude

". . . seventy-two labors brought us this food."
— from a Zen meal chant

The parcel on our doorstep has baked
all afternoon in the Southern California sun.
It's from the folks, from their boundless
generosity: two new shirts, two blouses for Arlie,
three towels, two bags of hazel nuts — and
a loaf of dark Lithuanian rye
(bread of my youth, bread of my ancestors!)
wrapped in a paper towel held
by an exhausted rubber band.
The loaf is dry as an adobe brick, and almost as heavy.

We appreciate my mother's endless supply
of clothes and towels and hazel nuts, but
I love this bread, this hard dry loaf,
seemingly stale and beyond saving,
but which I'll resurrect with the old peasant
trick of a sprinkling of water
and ten minutes in a warm oven.

Miracle bread, never molding,
never too old to rise again,
re-born now on our table among
the cheeses, eggs, jams — and the ghosts of
all the hands that brought them here.

Her Kitchen

in memoriam, KORNELIA SKRZYNECKI

Essential and sacred space
where body and soul,
two sides of one mystery,
were nourished by the food
of her hands', her heart's making.

How she moved on that intimate
and anonymous stage, unknown
at the city's edge, turning
like a dancer among
fridge and stove and table.

How she guided the transformation
of the day's bounty —
the backyard vegetables and eggs,
the morning milk — into
the precious bodies
of her family and friends.

There was no hiding
in that small place where
the western light poured in through
the one window above the sink.

We left her table
bellies filled, rounder,
soul-satisfied, more
who we were than
who we were when
first we entered.

Shirt

Perhaps you've noticed it hanging
in the closet,
sleeves empty,
unbuttoned, slack, inert —
or perhaps you've seen it
(not so often these days)
dancing in wind
on a clothesline, dancing like
a village idiot, billowing and filling
like a sail going nowhere.
More likely you've picked it up
from the laundry (medium starch) pressed
in among its fellows ready for wearing.
I know you've admired its colors,
the way the pockets slant
just so, the texture
of its textiles, the feel of it
on your back,
the reminder
it gives you of your body,
its bright, warm shell.

Tadpoles, Bass Hill, Circa 1953

The local ponds are full of recent spring rainwater
and teem with tadpoles wriggling among the reeds.
My friend and I are ankle deep in the water's clay edge,
our mothers' metal strainers in our hands.
We are scooping out tadpoles,
                    pouring them into glass jars.

Days later in the home-made aquarium
                    with its rocks and reeds,
back legs drop miraculously
from the ends of the tadpoles translucent,
                    iridescent bodies, each
with its concentric coil of pulsing intestines.

In another day, the front legs appear, stubs with wide apart
digits like startled hands.
Floating, tails down, noses above water,
the tadpoles have transformed into air-breathers,
the mystery of a billion years of evolution enacted
on the shelf in a boy's bedroom as the afternoon sun
streams through the glass.

Three tadpole survivors
(many have died and been scooped out)
have now dropped their tails and are clinging to the rocks
that poke above the water.

Only one frog makes it to his full froginess
and sits above the water on his rock like a little Buddha.
He even meets your gaze with his.

Speaking of the Ineffable

for B.P.

This is what she said: "I can't describe what happened,
only that afterward, for a brief while, everything was
   different.
One moment I was an ordinary woman taking a shower,
                                        the next,
something like a huge solar wind
washed through me. For a second I was not there—
though something that knew I wasn't was—then I was again,
but what that was was all of it, the shower, the water,
something
indescribably joyous . . . ."

And then again she said, "In that space between
sleep and waking, I became aware of a deep
and joyous satisfaction, as if
I were suckling at the very breast of Mother Universe.
I can't describe the taste except to say
it was the very essence of sweetness . . . ."

Though we can't, still we must speak of it,
must look down at the trembling finger,
                            fleshy and human, pointing
dumbly at the moon, glorious in all its practiced shining.
Back and forth, finger to moon, moon to finger,
like children, both our legs dangling uneasily
over the rickety fence of metaphor.

Half-Baked Sonnet

In form's warm oven
this dough's still moist,
only half risen.
The cook who'll foist

this loaf on his friends —
beware, he offends
without amends.

Working for Mr. Alo,
the Greengrocer

At thirteen, I learned how to greet customers,
how to sell vegetables and fruits,
how to fill up paper sacks with potatoes or green beans,
weigh them in the hanging scale.
I learned how to grasp the sacks,
flip and twist them a couple of times
quickly, leaving them with little ears at the corners.

I learned how to apply arithmetic,
adding, subtracting, multiplying the shillings and pence
in my head or with the pencil stub I kept
behind my ear. I learned the flash of shame
at miss-calculating a customer's bill
and how to apologize.
I learned how to sweep and mop a floor,
arrange a pyramid of apples or oranges,
how to tell when passion fruit was ripe.

I learned how to unload a produce truck at dawn
when the boss arrived from market,
and how to stack empty crates.

I learned a weariness at the end of the day
different from the pleasant exhaustions of boyhood play.
I learned about the hand-to-hand exchange
of metal and paper, the inexplicable
commerce of adult life, its endless
flow of food and money.

I learned about the progression of light and shade
through long days among the suchness
of artichokes and tangerines
and the long fragile row
of cordial bottles perched
on the highest shelf behind the counter.

I learned the hands of the clock on the Greengrocer's wall
were just like the ones in school — sometimes
they stopped, sometimes leapt forward.

I learned of daily ripeness and decay,
how everything left and returned —
days, vegetables, fruit, money, people.
Everything came back,
but never exactly
as it had been.

On the Edge, Still

Homeless, out of work, down-and-out,
as the previous generation used to say,
come to the end of his westward journey,
his American pilgrimage,
odyssey, American Dream, up against it,
up against the pleasure boats,
the white-winged elegant yachts
crossing back and forth across the waters
of the harbor, and beyond, the blue Pacific
like an impossible bowl of blue soup,
with no job in sight,
this man sits down at last
on the rocks by the water's edge
and stares at the small
waves tugging with their small fingers
at the skirts of North America.

Behind him, the tourists stroll, pockets fat
with the green and crinkly, wallets bulging.
The man almost swoons, sinks into hopelessness.
Where, but in his own insubstantial thoughts,
is his next meal?
The water laps at his feet.
The ocean is kissing the continent,
a celebration—a greeting and parting all at once,
and not just here, he imagines,
but all up and down the coast,
every coast, every continent
and island. There is no omega point
for this celebration, or for any dream.
When the world makes love to itself
among all its terrors and failures,
where is there room for his problems? Still,
no money is leaping into his pockets,
and mystical visions
will not feed the body.

Tourists continue to meander behind him.
Perhaps some notice the wild-haired man
sitting quietly on a rock, staring
down at his feet by the water;
they ease him out
beyond the edge
of their viewfinders,
those who notice him at all.

Absent-mindedly, the man lifts a stone,
about the size of a nice loaf of rye,
places it on top of another.
It rolls off. He replaces it. This time
adjusts it so it stays — two rocks,
one atop the other, silent and still
in a moving world of waves
and boats, gulls and clouds, dogs
and people. He scans the immediate area
around him, picks up another stone, a big one,
oddly shaped
like a large and awkward
slice of marble cake.
He sets it carefully atop the two —
on its point,
tries to find the fulcrum, the stillness,
working patiently with both hands,
backing-and-forthing against two sides of stone
in precise adjustments, like a man prolonging
his lover's ecstasy.
Ah, this is what his two hands are for,
to find this still point,
this point of balance,
this place of complete cessation,
that which *holds* the pendulum-swinging world.

continued

An hour passes.
He removes his hands from the stone.
The stone stays.

The three stones are no stiller than they ever were.
Their stillness now has a human quality,
stillness of desperation,
of nights without sleep, stillness of hope,
a stillness that will not last.
The man constructs another multilith
next to the first.
It takes him most of the afternoon,
but now the meandering tourists stop
to stare, drawn momentarily into the stillness.
Someone calls to the man: "Hey, Buddy," waves a five-dollar
bill, sets it on the sea wall,
weighs it down with a pebble.

Like a tip-jar on a coffee counter,
the bill attracts more money
and more tourists follow
suit, lay down their coins and bills.
Suddenly, the anonymous man has a job, a part to play
in the great theater of the economy, is a member
of the workforce again,
has an identity, has accidentally
reinvented his life here on the Coast of Reinventions.

Days later, a cardboard collection box appears
with snapshots for sale of the artist's Balanced Rock
Creations, the amount of the "donation" left
to the viewer's judgment. A one-page printed bio appears,
recounts the Balancer's long-time interest in Art,
his having fallen
on Hard Times,
his Persistence in the Face of Adversity.
(Someone is now his Agent!)
Through the days, the dollar bills flutter on the sea
wall like skewered butterflies.

For days, the man works at the slow and patient job
of balancing things on their edges,
his back to the people who pause
and stare and move on, he divinely indifferent
to the collection box, the slow accumulation
of the precious cash
that supports his life in this world.

The Artist's Job

According to Kafka's diary,
"The artist's task is to lead
the isolated individual
into the infinite life."

So here we go, Friend — I presume
you're as isolated as I am
(but, ahem, I'm an artist) —
take my hand and let us head

for heaven together, noting
please that homeless and out-of-work
veteran — so he signs — on the corner.
Yes, it's OK to part with a buck

for his sake, since we haven't yet
been able to stop those pesky wars
that have all but scrambled
his remaining sense of self-worth . . . .

Step this way, the Infinite is just down
this alley, just by the garbage cans.
Mind the broken bottles,
that suspicious puddle of ooze.

If you find joy unaccountably
rising in your throat, it's OK, give
voice to it now: "Oh, we are marching
to Pretoria, Pretoria . . . ."

On the way to Paradise
we may be blessed
by its harbingers, those "foretastes" of
the Primordial Absolute . . . . This is

as it should be, as circumstances
have a way of tamping down the Infinite, though
never completely. Here we are now
under a pergola of autumn trees stretching

all the way to the next century

and beyond. Ah, this dusty country road,
isn't it quiet and noble, my Friend?
Look at the pebbles clustered

all along the shoulder, the soggy trench
and its croaky frogs. Surely, Spring
is here now, can you feel it rising
through the soles of our bare feet?

Let's rest by this pond, shall we?
I feel spent from this taxing artist's work,
and, after all, a lifetime has gone by
since first I hired on for this.

Let me soak my gnarly toes here among
the reeds and tadpoles. You, too,
Friend, drop your worries here, rest
a while, before you go on without me.

Bird Song

for PETER SKRZYNECKI

My friend, in pain from collapsed
marriage, collects the brightly
colored birds from the backyard aviary
built with his own hands and
that will not survive the divorce.
He ushers them into hand cages,
takes them back to the bird seller —
all, that is, but the insanely gorgeous
Gouldian finches, a set
of three paired mates.
Those he drives to Rookwood Cemetery
and, in a solitary ritual of tears and anguish
among the headstones in the Polish section,
opens the cage door:
First the males, then the females
fly out, head straight for the nearby
branches of a Stringy Bark,
and pause there, perhaps confounded
at their suddenly cageless
lives among the quietest of inhabitants.

Years later, at my friend's parents'
graveside, he and I stand
in the silence of a weekday afternoon.
In that still City of the Dead,
the only sound,
a distant finch's song.

Opening the Heart

for CHARLOTTE JOKO BECK, *Zen teacher*

Those with the eyes in which you can see
for a thousand miles have always urged us
to soften and open our hearts.
So much hardens the heart. We build such fortresses
out of the leavings of what we can't or won't accept.

Of course, they know we know in the end
the heart will be opened,
whether by that last grief we can't choke down, or
that one pebble accidentally kicked
against the bamboo pole, or by the surgeon's saw
parting our ribs in a ceremony of blood and steam.

Still, they urge us not to wait, to open
now — always now — always right in the middle
of all our best reasons not to:
                    in the middle of our righteous anger,
our comfortable boredom,
the unjustified — unjustifiable — pain visited upon us.

"Open to it all," their clear, calm eyes say.
"There's no way out, only a way through.
The path is a razor's edge. The heart is not a fist.
Where is the pain when the one asking has disappeared?"

We hear it again and again. Simple. Clear. And we forget
it again and again. So we sit and stand and walk —
over and over — until eventually we discover
we really are sitting and standing and walking,
and the thousand other things we were doing
fall away a little.

The wagon train of fear around our hearts begins
to break up. Between the wagons
we see our occasional fierce warrior
heading full-tilt towards us, and beyond him
a lot of fascinating prairie, a lot of open sky.

The Western Felt Works

Early 1960s in the Manic Industrial Heart
of Chicago's Southside

for VIC GUDAITIS

Three infernal summers spent among the torturous itch
of wool fibers, skin-eating, rash-raising acids,
and labor-bent men and women resigned
to death-in-life; I was the cocky college kid
who knew he could walk out the gate for another year —
eventually forever — just before Labor Day weekend.

My first summer there, my father's friend, Vic —
may his soul rest in peace — was my mentor and partner
on the fulling machine.

We stood opposite each other across the machine's open pit
with its endlessly tumbling yards of balled-up felt,
pounded by the fulling hammers — the racing thump
of the industrial heart measuring out
the finite beats of its own passing.

The two of us, like some parody
                        of a domestic couple working with
laundered bed sheets, stretched the felt between us, pulling
the soapy, acidic creases out of the edges as thousands of feet
of fulled felt rolled up and out and coiled onto the turning
spindle above our heads spraying us with acid drops
as heavy as any summer shower.

At the end of that first day,
I was sure my fingerprints had worn off.
Later, in the cutting department, I saw workers who'd
sacrificed fingers to machines that stamped
gaskets and washers out of the hard, dry felt sheets.

This was Hell, I thought, Dante's *Inferno*
(which I'd been studying in European Lit.)
These people were damned, and so was I
but only to a summer's Purgatory:
I would walk away with fat pockets,

my youth intact, unbroken by machines
                              and the dreadful hours
of overtime, nothing but prospects ahead down the long,
leisurely road
of my dazzling life.

Looking back, I see Vic, the one who showed me
what it meant to transcend
by going through resignation.
He was calm, if not joyful, stoic —
a survivor. I see him clearly now, thirty years later, eating
his one lunch sandwich, made by himself in his lonely
kitchen, chewing deliberately, sipping coffee,
later smoking his one Lucky Strike.

To him, raised on back-breaking farm work —
plowing, sowing, scything fields of rye by hand
                              late into the night —
who had made it through the War, had suffered through
untold dislocations and privations —
cartings off to Siberian Camps, hunger,
the deaths of wife and parents —
what was a little factory work, a little labor
here at the tail-end of the Industrial Age,
day in and day out, for the rest of his short life?

The Christian Brothers

*"Each man has only one genuine vocation
— to find the way to himself."*

— HERMAN HESSE

Brother pulled me aside one day
before rugby practice,
fixed me with his clear eye,
asked if I'd ever considered
a vocation,
from the Latin *vocare*, to call.

Perhaps I was one of the chosen,
summoned by God to do his work,
to be a priest, perhaps a brother,
to minister to the sick or teach the young,
join the holy missions
in Africa, South America,
or perhaps till the fields quietly
in some abbey in Kentucky or France,
high on black bread and water,
speaking rarely, ecstatic in silence.

Brother, in his rugby shorts,
on bony, pale legs.
Brother on the sideline exhorting
us as we crushed together in scrums
and fell in piles of laughing, groaning
pimply-faced, fuzz-lipped, horny male
adolescents. Brother, loping past us
as we ran our laps.

Brothers in their black habits,
cassocks swirling as they rode
the Holy Ghost through school —
hall, stair, court, field.

Brothers of the golden, holy voices, chanters
of the *Tantum Ergo Sacramentum*.
(We mocked them with
"Tantum ergo
makes your hair grow.
Vene remor
makes it stay more.
Et antiquum
makes you handsome . . . ."

Brothers of the black leather strap
that danced in twos and fours and sixes
on our upturned, trembling palms.
Brothers of Latin conjugations and French declensions.
(*amo, amas, amat* . . . .
j'aime, tu aimes, il aimes . . . .

Brothers who marched us off to Confession, Communion.
(*Forgive me, Father, for I have sinned.*
It has been seven days since my last confession,
and since that time I have committed six impure thoughts
and three impure deeds . . . .
Brothers who Confirmed us and Retreated us and sat us
in the medieval incense forests of Benediction.
Brothers of the fear of damnation in eternity.
Brothers of the doctrine *mens sano in corpore sano*.
Brothers of the wood shop who taught us
how to chisel, fit, and glue crucifixes
and build small balsa-wood shrines to the Blessed Virgin.
Brothers of Geometry, Trigonometry
                              and the laws of numbers,
the angles (obtuse, acute, and right),
Brothers of the Logarithm and the intersecting planes.

continued

Brothers of the Periodic Table
and the miracle of fizzing phosphorous —
burning, consuming the water.
Brothers of the pure purple Bunsen-burner flame.
Brothers of Force and Mass and Acceleration.
Brothers of Logos and Poetry, Shakespeare and Dickens,
worlds within worlds within worlds —
Puck and Pip, Bottom and Oliver.
Brothers who confiscated our girlie magazines,
and spoke of masturbation
without ever naming it.
Brothers of the pure and impure thought and deed.
Brothers of hairbreadth, hare-brained theological
distinctions, inane Aquinases
of the precise boundary between
venial and mortal sin.
Brothers of Hell and Heaven, Purgatory and Limbo.
Brothers whom I loved and feared.
Brothers of report cards ("Algy is quite bright
but should apply himself
more diligently to his studies.")
Brothers of the grand explorers:
the Raleighs and Drakes, da Gamas and Hartogs,
the Scots and Cooks.

Brothers of the Never-Never, of the Old Sod,
of years of British and European history, of monastic
stones sinking inch by inch into the earth.
Brothers of the Stations of the Cross, and the Missal, and
the Breviary, and the Apostles' Creed,
the Perfect Act of Contrition,
and the Litany of the long days of our youth.

The Candle on the Urinal,
New Delhi

After a steaming day of temples, mosques, pillars and towers, we return to the Hotel Rajdoot. I go into the "Gents" on the ground floor. There's been a power outage. The only light in the cavernous space comes from a burnt-down candle on top of the urinal. It pushes its small light against the looming walls and ceiling. I step up to the unexpected altar, present myself to the glowing porcelain and watch, as if for the first time again, the sacred water flow.

On Turning Down a Gift of Guns

for my father-in-law, Colonel FLOYD DAVID WILLIAMS
US Army Retired. (1920-2002)

Colonel, it was a gesture I appreciated, the proffered gifts, your service .45, the Japanese Nambu, the collector's .38, the shotguns, the deer rifles. And part of me was tempted, that part that remembers a dry Ohio afternoon in summer when on the farm of a distant aunt, met for the first time, I was allowed, even encouraged, to "try out" the guns left by her deceased husband, my never-met distant uncle.

I was fifteen, newly-arrived from Australia, my head filled with American movies, mostly cowboys and Chicago tough-guys, and I had always wanted my own gun — say a .22, or even a good quality BB-rifle would have done the trick. But no, my father was opposed to guns. While I lived in his house, there would be no guns . . . no motorcycles, no smoking, no trying out for the high school football team, either. After I moved out, I could do as I wished.

But for this one glorious afternoon, there were guns! More than I'd seen in one place together this side of a museum, and little boxes of lethal ammunition heavy as gold ingots. Out behind the barn, my Aunt Julia and I set up beer cans and bottles, and the shooting began.

I fired a .32 silver-plated revolver, the only one my aunt kept loaded in the house, right above the kitchen sink in front of the dinner dishes. I fired an assortment of .22 target pistols — revolvers and automatics. I shot a lethal looking .38 police special with a kick I can still bring up in body memory, and I turned out to be a pretty good shot, nailed a beer can three times in a row with a .22 six-shooter. And with an ancient double-barreled shotgun and a sexy deer-rifle we added more holes to the forty-gallon drum for burning trash.

32

There we were, a middle-aged Ohio farm-woman and a fifteen year-old new immigrant: we must have fired off five hundred rounds between us! My ears rang for an hour afterwards and I can still smell the cordite, gunpowder, and hot oil. We obliterated a few six-packs' worth of empty beer cans and shattered a dozen or more brown bottles. Auntie Julia liked guns, and I did too, that day, but the excess of it got to me, somehow, or it must have because I don't actually remember thinking that to myself, that is, my fifteen-year-old self didn't say, "The excess of this is getting to me." Yet, after that day, I lost my desire to own a gun, almost without being aware of it. Frankly, now the sons of bitches scare me. Even when they're empty, I never really believe it!

So, I'm truly grateful for the offer, knowing its value coming from an old soldier. The two Samurai swords you "liberated from a couple of dead Japs"? Yeah, sure, I'd be happy to accept those.

Rush-Hour Lament

You're stopped in a Sargasso Sea
of GM-Toyota-Ford-Mercedes flotsam and jetsam
becalmed, though far from calm.
For the ten-thousandth time, you recall
"Life as it is, the only teacher," and you take a deep breath,
sigh, and come back to the little world
of your car's interior, the wonder of the instruments,
the CD putting out Glenn Gould's version of Bach's
Keyboard Concerto No. 3,
its joyful energy, a torrent
of complex melody and harmony. For a moment
you're happy,
but you're also human
and you can't quite reconcile that happiness
with this mess we've created,
this imploding system
all around you, closing its spiked walls
around your life even as it bathes you in celestial music.
The woman in the lane next to you
progresses at the same non-rate. She drums
her elegant long fingernails
as her bladder, like yours, slowly fills.
You're in your metal and plastic straight-jacket,
arms pinned to a wheel,
steering straight ahead, rolling on rubber wheels, each one
a tapped-out tree, one less alveolus in the world's lungs.
You feel like some reverse Kurz
at the end of the Industrial River,
not "darkest Africa," but shiniest America,
the river of laws and greed, of drugged consumption,
of accumulating and discarding,
a parody of gluttony, gorging and cacking
in your own backyard, in your own pants,
like a babbling, innocent child, smearing it around
and calling it good.

Oh, myth of the Freeway, myth of the two-way river!
We flow down in the morning,
flow back at night, toting our Toyota barge,
our Ford ferry, and we think
we've gone out and returned,
when we've just gone out and further out
further from home.

Anno Domini

Would you like to step in and see the *testa* of *Santa Caterina*?
A painting of Saint Catherine's head?
No, the *testa* of Saint Catherine.
You mean a bust of Saint Catherine's head?
No, her head.
A fresco?
No, no, her head, her actual head, her
head, you know, in *mummificazione*!
Oh my God, her mummified dead head?
Yes, *giustamente*, in this church, the *Basilica di San Domenico*,
right here before us, here
on the edge of our old Siena.

Please to step forward.
There, on the right side of the *navata*
you can see the *Capella di Santa Caterina* where
our treasured saint's head sits . . .
wedged in its gothic mini-temple-shaped reliquary
like Alice in the rabbit's house,
white-whimpled, lids closed and sunken over
eyeless sockets, stretched parchment skin, rat-gnarled
nose, wizened mouth, two buck teeth . . . .

She is waiting *pazientemente* since 1380 for
the Last Judgment, *il Giudizio Universale,* when her scattered
bones and *unghia,* how you say, fingernails
(and her one finger preserved
on the other side of the nave,
long-nailed, pointing straight up)
and her *preziosa* locks of hair shared
                              among the many *basilica d' Italia*
making the *cura miracolosa,* answering the *petizione* endless,
large and small . . .

as now, perhaps, for the young man
stylish to a T
kneeling in our day, our year, 2001 anno domini,
in front of her, his face raised, lips parted, trembling, tears
flowing down his face, yes, in 2001 anno domini . . . .

Over here, above the *altare,* you see the famous painting
by Sodoma of the Saint in her *svenimento,* how you say
 in *inglese,* in her swoon *mistica . . . .*

Nozze mistiche by Il Sodoma
(GIOVANNI ANTONIO BAZZI)
1477 – 14 February 1549

Contemporary Ancient Poem

Sitting near the spice garden,
I watch the budding flowers
move in wind. The chime rings
three notes again and again.

In the distance,
hills appear through mist—
or is it smog, or, smoke drifting
south from the L.A. riots?

Li Po! Tu Fu!
Twelve-hundred years later,
I read your words,
true then, true now.

Injustice, fear, anger, death.
A spider on its thread,
the song of birds.
Has anything changed?

The Given Necessary

And what if we could hold each
moment of our life as a gift,
a necessary gift?
Gift because it comes unbidden,
necessary because how can you argue
against simple *isness*?
Any one who's tried has always
failed. Who was it said philosophy
is a painted door on the wall of reality?
Painted, never to be opened by
thought, no matter how brilliant, just
an image of a door on a wall.
Thinking won't get you through
that wall, perhaps a good koan might, after
it has driven you almost crazy, maybe
let you see at last, as Rumi did,
that we've been pounding
on the wall from the inside,
or even better, that there
never was any wall.

Down Dead Cold Enlightened Blues

Rainy night
Stuffed head
Cold in the nose
Should be in bed

Aching bones
Tired feet
Droopy eyes
Need to sleep

Itchy throat
Pain in the chest
Hacking cough
Gotta rest

No way out
Miles from home
Gotta work
Can't go home

Can't go home
Gotta stay
Feel like shit
Need the pay

Need the pay
Gotta eat
Gotta live
Life is sweet

Life is sweet
Ain't no doubt
Even sickness
Brings it out

Brings it out
Bring it out
Nothin' to do
Sing and shout

Sing and shout
Shout and sing
Dance a dance
And do a thing

Do your thing
And let it ring
Let it ring
Let it ring

Blow my nose
Blow my mind
Hack up phlegm
I don't mind

I don't mind
I don't care
Nowhere to go
No one there

No one there
No one here
No one anywhere
No one nowhere

Just a cold
In the nose
Just a cold
Who knows

Where it's from
Who knows
How it came
Where it goes

How it goes
Nose to nose
No one knows

Domestic Aubade

A calendar hangs on a nail,
its top page a photograph of bare trees
in presumably February snow
trembling in the breeze of warm air
from the vent above.

A dozen books line up on a shelf,
squeezed by non-twin ceramic vases,
improvised book ends,
a motely platoon of partisans
of some lost cause in mismatched uniforms.

A round clock floats above the fireplace,
its one red secondhand twitching
its circuit, ever chasing the now,
lonely knitting needle, finding neither
partner nor skein of wool.

A faux Tiffany lamp casts real
light onto the desk's flat surface,
a lake of white paper, where a black pen
walks across, flies back, more miraculous even
than Jesus. Walks across, flies back.

My Mother and The Wheel of Fire

If coaxed, my mother will tell the story
of the wheel of fire from her girlhood
on her parents´ farm in Lithuania.
But you must coax her
for the telling details, urge her to recall
the sequence of events, and
as in all the best stories, you
must take it on yourself, wear it, fill
it, sacrifice a portion of your
own life for its sake.

One mid-summer day, when my mother
was ten years old, she was left at the farm
while the rest of the family
went off to Sunday mass.
Somehow, she had hurt her foot
with a handsaw, and now it was swathed in bandages.

They left her in charge of a younger boy,
the son of one of the tenants,
a Petrukas or Vincukas —
diminutives for Peter and Vincent — she can't
remember which. Her stern but loving father
(the grandfather I never knew) told her
not to leave the house, not to go gallivanting
around on her injured foot.

When the family — all the five sisters and one brother
and two parents — and the rest of the household
piled into the wagons and left for church,
my mother soon grew restless.
She decided she and Petrukas or Vincukas
would go pick flowers

continued

So, off they went to a nearby fallow field
full of waving daisies, she hobbling
on her bandaged foot, urging along the innocent
and now faceless Petrukas or Vincukas.
It was a hot day, and as they wandered farther
and farther from the house, the bouquets
of daisies growing in their hands,
they didn't notice the mushrooming storm clouds
until it was too late.

The wind suddenly picked up,
everything grew dark, and the lightning
began its primeval dance.
My mother looked towards the farmhouse
and saw a haystack catch fire,
apparently struck by lightning.

She began running to the farmhouse in fright,
her bandages unraveling, the younger
boy trailing behind her.

Then, as she tells it,
there was a tremendous clap of thunder
("Perkunas" as we say in Lithuanian,
both the word for thunder
and for the pagan god of thunder).
Petrukas or Vincukas cried out,
my mother stopped, turned, and witnessed
what she calls a Wheel of Fire
that rolled furiously along the ground
like a blazing bicycle wheel.
It seemed to run over or through
the boy, knocking him flat
on his back and singeing his hair and clothes.

He lay there, clothes smoking,
as my mother, terrified, ran back to him,
knelt and beat his smoldering shoulders
with her bare hands.

What happened next, she can't
remember exactly, but some farmhands
who had been bathing in the nearby river
ran up and attended the boy, now
conscious but dazed, and carried him
into the garden near the house.
There, they dug a shallow trough,
lay him in it and buried him
up to his neck, his head
sticking out of the sod like some cabbage.
They did this to "draw off" the electricity
or the power of Perkunas
that had entered him —
all this, of course, in accordance
with the folk customs of that place and time.

The boy recovered, my mother was punished
for having disobeyed her father, and everyone
almost managed to talk
her out of her experience, suggesting
there was no Wheel of Fire, that it was lightning
after all, or something that had fallen
from the burning haystack.

But when my mother tells this story,
she gets what I call her "gypsy face," that expression
half fearful, half knowing
with eyes that are focused on a place
a few light years behind you,
a place you can't see
but have strong reason to suspect is there nonetheless.

So that's the story of my mother,
Petrukas or Vincukas, and the Wheel of Fire.
It happened a long time ago
on my grandfather's farm in Lithuania,
right here on Planet Earth.

By the Numbers

I'm tired of being Number One.
On second thought,
this is the third time I've said it:
it's the Fourth Way for me.
But please hand me that fifth of scotch.
I have a sixth sense for these things,
being the seventh son of a seventh son.
I'm heading for the Eightfold Path,
gonna go the whole Nine Yards, too!

The Man Who Had Singing Fits

He would begin unexpectedly
anywhere, bubbling
into song at the Woolworth's
cash register, in the elevator,
the restaurant
as the waitress approached with coffee,
in board meetings.

The pale canary of his heart chirped
from its cage
while all around him
we woke momentarily, startled
out of our cultural trance,
too amazed to be embarrassed.

We, his family and friends,
used to these fits, we too
became charmed,
the soft voice, the lilting, gentle song
that never quite made sense,
had something to do
with a quiet, confused love.

He would sing for half a minute,
then he'd be back,
no memory of his departure
or return, no memory
of the stream he'd dipped us into,
that one running along just under
the surface of anything
you and I think we understand.

A Different Life

Say, instead of your suburban tract house
here in Southern California
you lived on a remote island in Indonesia,
your house in a tree, one hundred and fifty feet
above the forest floor, your first act each morning
before your feet touched Mother Earth,
the careful and conscious descent
down a series of connected, notched poles,
the family dog slung
under your arm, a spear in hand,
your bare toes gripping
the carved steps, everything swaying
in what wind there might be.
You descend with attention from sleep and domesticity
to earth — the slightest slip could find you dead
on the duff, sightless eyes staring
at the forest canopy.

Or is this Noble Savage life also steeped in dull habit?
For you, life-time tree-dweller, no learned fear
of heights, is this jungle life just routine, as in
another life, your token two-way glance
at the stop sign as you roll through,
coffee mug in hand
on your way to work, lost once more
in the dream
you call your life?

Postcard from Home

Sitting on the deck, bare feet
on the railing, I watch and listen
to this day spilling out
its myriad flow of details,
one after another,
one on top of the other,
seamlessly,
with no apologies,
not the slightest backing
off: two ruby-throated humming
birds drinking their sugar water,
distant dogs barking, the sudden shriek
of wood torn
by a neighbor's power saw,
those boulders poking out
of the hillside, another
subdivision going up
on the stripped land
across the valley.
Each detail says, "This!"
and has always and ever
only said, "This!"

Near Šunskai, Lithuania

On my father's ancestral farm near the village
where only the church like a bright jewel dropped
and lost in a field, remains unchanged,
we find a woman, Birutė, and her ancient father,
the one who bought the place
from my father's father over fifty years ago.

Half the original house still stands,
the other half added over the long years
of my father's exile. The outbuildings
are not the same, the grove
is the same grove, but not the same
oaks, birches, lindens.

The field of half-grown rye
barely moves in midsummer
late morning. The original well is dry.
We look into it as into a place
in ourselves long abandoned,
see the round hollow shape,
the curved stone and earth wall.

Chickens, ducks, and geese
wander around the yard,
the 45th generation of descendants
of the ones who provided eggs and meat
for my father's boyhood body.
The black rooster calls his hens and chicks
to something he's unearthed under a bush,

and they all carry on with their lives, unconcerned
about the humans strolling the property, pilgrims
looking for roots, for the past,
for something. Birutė tells us she
and her 90-year old father
work the farm alone,
her husband having hanged himself
three years earlier. She tells us,
as she hand-cranks a bucket of water up
from the new well, that life is hard.

50

She tells us in a direct, uncomplaining way,
simply stating a given.
She is ruddy-cheeked and healthy looking
except for a set of bad teeth.
My father tries to give her some dollars. She refuses.
Well, sell us some eggs, he says,
and against her wishes he insists on paying
three times their price.

Just before we leave, after wishing each other
good fortune and God's blessings (there's a priest
in our group), my mother takes a drink
from the bucket with an old tin cup.
She suddenly seems to grow taller
as she praises the water, its taste, its coolness.

Perhaps this water that she
now drinks, drawn up from fifty feet
below the earth's surface, perhaps
this same water came down as rain
in my mother's youth — why not even on the same day,
the first day my father brought her home
to meet his parents, and his father charmed
and amazed my mother with his fiddle playing

and his fabled story-telling, and that silly trick
he was famous for among the children
of the region, where he would laugh uproariously
and then, passing his hand down over his face,
stop abruptly, and freeze his face
into stone for a few seconds
until the children started to get

edgy, and then he'd smile and tickle their ribs
and play them another song or tell them
another story, perhaps the one about
the time he encountered the Devil
when he was mushrooming in the forest
and had lost his way.

Growing Up Double

At the end of their refugee journey,
the long forced pilgrimage, burdened
with the smallest and heaviest bundles,
they settle at last, uneasily,
in the wounded heart of a city
or its distant fringes beyond
the fashionable and complacent suburbs.

The small children learn
the unspoken rules of a double life:
Here, in the father's domain,
the old ways are preserved: chickens
slaughtered in the back yard, the mother
tongue enforced, though the children
are already beginning to speak it
with strange new accents
that grate on their parents' ears.

Outside the father's door,
in the streets and schoolyards of the new world,
the immigrant children soon speak like locals,
are re-baptized
by their new friends with new names.
They will respond to two names,
will carry them both
for separate occasions.

In the homes of their new playmates,
they see what they never see under their own roofs —
animals treated like people (dogs
and cats at table), or possessions
treated with indifference
by those who never had to turn their backs
and walk quickly away
with only the suddenly precious
contents of their own pockets.

To be human, of course, is to adjust
to almost anything, and the children grow
into their double lives
gracefully and easily.
After all, it may not be
that much more difficult
to cultivate two identities than one—and
in the end, even
a little easier to see through.

At the Imperial War Museum,
London, 1995

Here are the engines of war, gathered and displayed,
cleansed of their mire and blood, only the smell
of oil clings—our century's signature—a hell
of wheels, rockets, wings, and armor plates.
In the great central hall, fighter planes
hang together in mid-bank. (You can tell
from their lack of weight they're engineless shells.)
One floor below, in the basement, fittingly placed,
a recreated trench from the Somme where you
may walk in awe through recreated sights,
sounds, and smells: distant gunfire, a slop pail
that actually stinks, the sizzle of eggs frying,
the mannequin soldiers, their faces blue
with cold and fear, the dirt under their nails.

Uncertainty

Uncertainty, the wallet
I stash in my back pocket,
stuffed with credit cards
from banks with no capital.
Uncertainty, the pen
scrawling my life.

Uncertainty, my lover,
bright woman of mystery,
rolling hips enticing
me onward — and upward.

Uncertainty, just beneath
the surface of the mundane,
inhabits our habits, un-
stitches the careful weave
of days, pulls the thread,
quite unravels us.

Uncertainty, our wife, our spouse,
our boon companion,
our priest and confessor,
our moral stockbroker, our
movie producer and director,
impresario of our daily lives.

Uncertainty, I embrace you now,
and regret
my infidelities
with Certainty, she,
who in the end
always betrayed me.

Once in India

turning the corner into the crowded marketplace
overwhelmed with the desire
to disappear from his own life, he wanted
to merge into that numberless crowd, hidden
in his white cotton garments, simply
wanted to walk away from himself.

For a moment, he believed
it was possible. By stepping off the path
he could take that other road that diverged — not
into a wood, but into a sea of humanity.

He did not leave his path —
because he saw
as if in one of those Moghul miniatures
painted with the single hair from the tail
of a small rodent, how his life
would continue as it had before:
it would still be *his* life,
perhaps more exotic and strange:
the pervasive and not unpleasant smell
of cow-dung cooking fires,
chappatis for dinner, sandals for his feet,
perhaps, if he were lucky, an authentic guru.
But *he* would still be there, *he* would not
escape through this strategy
the thick and cloying presence of himself.

The only Way was through his life
as it occurred moment by moment — the quiet
times of zazen on the cushion, the chaos of mad desires,
the insanities of work and relationships. He finally
had to embrace it all — and not once and for all —
but over and over: He had to BE the LIFE that he already
and always was just as it manifested....

The marketplace arose within him,
                    its sari-ed women, mangoes,
papayas, the blue diesel fumes cloying mouth and lungs,
                                    the rattle
of three-wheeled cabs and tinkling bicycle bells
and for just a moment he knew
there was nowhere to go nor any need to escape
this prison of no bars and no walls.

Phosphenes and Mother Light

When you're startled from darkness into light,
or when you rub your eyes,
those lights you see are your own pattern.
From whence that cellular fire,
those stored up bits of sunlight,
Shakespeare's star-stuff,
from what light of light,
from what Mother Light?

Rendered on the page, they look
like the profane language of comic strips,
the unreadable but clear typescript of swearing,
or what cartoon characters see
when they're hit on the head.
Fifteen distinct types.
You have one all your own.

Why precisely fifteen?
Why twelve signs of the zodiac?
Nine points of the Enneagram? Why
three somatotypes? Fifty-two cards
in a Bicycle deck? Why four seasons
(let alone the four quadrants of the Kosmos),
seven days in a week,
twenty-four hours, ten fingers and toes,
up and down, inside and out?

In the thirteenth century,
when they asked Dogen Zenji
what he brought back from China, he replied,
"Eyes horizontal, nose vertical,"
and we've been debating his meaning ever since,
as if we could ever explain the mystery,
as if we could ever explain the obvious.

Staying Put

For years, it was my job
to move on.
Now my job, it seems, is

to stay put.
Before, novelty
and adventure were my

daring friends, sparkling,
many-faceted.
Now, I'm accompanied

by a gentleman,
a little dour
in his gray suit,

who refuses
excitement, nostalgia,
the lure of romance,

who tugs at his neatly
creased slacks, adjusts
the mauve rag sinking

in his breast pocket
and sits down to wait —
no, to attend.

Lines

lines
of
only
one
word
per
line
one
word
in
a
line
sad
skinny
poem
reed
blowing
in
wind
going
nowhere
fast

two words
per line
feels better
feels stronger
arm wrestling
a contest
of strength
a dance
a jig
who knows
what mood
the poet
might fall
or rise
into

perhaps three words
per precious line
three glittering words
agate opals emeralds
not dull stones
glowing incandescent pearls
strung on string
around a neck
beauty on beauty
foreground and background
a delightful threesome
worth of words
Truth Beauty Art
Buddha Dharma Sangha
I we it

for health joy celebration
and that quatro feeling
of boxiness and constraint
self-imposed disciplined impulse
kept and caught tight
four-cornered balanced boundaries
field of ordered play
don't ask how large
freedom's own self-restraint
tightly bound already free
co-arising four quadrants
of the holonic Kosmos
nowhere to go

but into the bliss pentagon
where five lives in freedom
and all flows with ease
and constraint sheds its coat
to warm zephyrs of delight
of words free to play
to cavort like new lambs
fresh from the universe

continued

onward, onward to lordly narrative sixes
Greek-like hexameters, Homer's salty realm
where story wants to come forward
the divine song-tales, god-stories
and the mysterious birth of myth
where sea spume fills the air
and heroes wander lost for years
with no end in sight

the poetry of home gone, nothing but the progress of endless
accumulation, of adventure, the hero growing in wisdom or
age, either way, lonesome for succor of distant home, for rest,
respite, peace, ecstatically lost in the arbitrary labyrinth
of prose.

Leaving Kaunas, 1944

(DITA remembers)

When, rattling downhill,
unable to make the corner, the wagon tipped over,
and all the luggage, clothes, shoes
scattered across lanes
where three streets met
and blocked cars, trucks, pedestrians —
Lithuanian and German
(as yet not Russian) —
and Ragažinis the wagon driver stood
thunderstruck, forgotten whip hanging from his hand,
while the mares Foggy and Blackie
lowered their heads calmly down,

only then did my mother whisper to me,
thinking in that moment
about her brother
who through a long exhausting day
had carefully loaded up
all those family possessions
and then with his new bride
mounted two bicycles
and started pedaling
the sixty kilometers to Marijampolis,
"Just don't blab to Kastytis
about what happened here."

My Father, at the Age of 83, Shows Up at the Family Reunion, Sporting an Amazing Beard

for KOSTAS ZOLYNAS

According to our mother
he looks like Santa Claus, but to me
he's more like a retired admiral, trailing
years of high-seas glories, or maybe
more like Poseidon himself,
lord of seas and waves,
the hidden depths of shade
and swaying seaweed
and bending light.

Is this the man
who brought me a single sweet
Jaw Breaker
each day after work,
who during the sun-drenched
summers of my boyhood
hand-clippered my hair down
to my sun burnt scalp,
who lost sleep over my adolescent
forays into the wild city night?

Now he looks like his own father,
that spade-bearded man
in the black and white snapshot
on my wall,
a farmer awkward in his Sunday suit,
a nineteenth-century man,
a fiddle-player and story teller,
old in the modern world
having outlived his time.

"I'm no longer fit for this planet,"
my father now says
when faced with the latest
technological marvel
or some piece of outrageous daily news,
his beard lending the sentence more authority.
And, despite my computer literacy,
my knowing the difference between
a high resolution TV and a low density disk,
my comfort with navigating
the World Wide Web, I feel myself edging
toward the place of his planet's discards,
that place where we look and listen and cast about us
and nothing seems familiar
but the distant call, quiet and insistent, heard
like the murmur of wind in grass
or the ocean breaking on a shore.

Recurring Dreams: The House

Never the house
of my waking
life—though always
familiar, its rooms,
its comfortable furnishings,
sometimes peeling paint
or a broken window,
a sink filled
with water—
the dream world, home . . .

until I find myself
in the back
section, in long forgotten
or never seen rooms
where I always sense
someone has just left.

Sometimes,
having passed
through the seldom-
used door,
I feel
like someone gone
a long time,
returning now
to an unmade bed,
a lamp glowing onto an open book,
a faint smell of distant
cooking, a dim shadow
crossing at the end
of the hallway.

Villanelle of the Iron Bell

The iron bell tolls the time; the time is now.
The past is dead; the future never here.
Is this all we know — indeed, need to know?

If truth is beauty, beauty truth, then how
we live that mystery helps us clearly hear
the iron bell toll the time; that time is now,

and nothing will bring back the whys or hows
of yesterdays; they are for us to bear.
That much we know. Why do we need to know

any more? If we could arise and bow
toward our limits, would we fret or care
that the iron bell tolls the time that is now?

And nothing we can try to do allows
it to be otherwise; thus we may dare
not to know — or else all we want to know

will stand between us and our lives. We'll go
farther from all that's truly near and dear.
The iron bell tolls the time; the time is now,
Surely, all we know — or can hope to know.

The Interruption

We were discussing "Song of Myself,"
had read aloud those lovely first lines
where Whitman directs us to assume what he assumes,
and I'd said that wasn't arrogance or egotism, rather
a compassionate humility because
every atom belonging to me as good belongs to you.

The class was reasonably attentive, ranging
from the engaged to the nearly unconscious,
when the door opened, and an upright human skeleton
crossed the threshold, dangling from a hook in its skull
attached to a high-tech aluminum gallows pole.
Stunned silence — an almost silence:
the yellow bones clacked and rattled quietly
like a bamboo wind chime heard from a neighbor's yard.

A live female head appeared
behind the skeleton as they both entered the room.
She apologized for the interruption and asked
if this was the room for the osteopathy demonstration.
I didn't know, I said, but never mind,
this literature class could always use
another student, even a late one.
The class laughed, she laughed, the skeleton grinned.

Well, the woman said, she'd just leave "Suzy"
in the front of the room in the corner
if that was all right with us. It was.
We all watched as the woman wheeled "Suzy"
down the aisle along the wall, Suzy-the-skeleton
dancing her little death-
dance all the way, fleshless hands clicking against fleshless
thighs, metatarsals jiggling together awkwardly
as if operated by an apprentice puppeteer.

The woman apologized once more,
exited stage-right. I walked over to the skeleton,
took hold of one of her metacarpals with one of my own.
It was not exactly like holding hands with Death,
more like in the ninth grade, at the sock hop, inviting
that frail wallflower to dance
because no one else had.
Her response, a fragile hand
barely warmer than those cool bones.

I wish I could say I unhooked "Suzy" and began dancing
there in front of the class, and that I spun her around
through a fox-trot or waltz, air swirling
through her vacant ribcage and empty pelvis,
and that the class picked up the beat, banging
their desks with pens and books
like Hollywood inmates in a penitentiary cafeteria,
and that someone began crooning a romantic dance tune
as I dipped her deeply and steered her along
with expert pressure from the palm of my right
hand on the back of her ribs — just
the way I didn't at those early dances
of awkward embraces, when to touch
the front of a ninth-grade female's body
with the front of my own was more than I could take
and all that I wanted.

Instead, I held the hand of Sister Suzy Death briefly,
enthralled by the intimacy of her bones, her grin
of real teeth, yellow and hard.
I remembered Whitman's fabled sensitivity to touch,
his being driven to ecstasy of delight
by the light touch of a lover's hand or even
by the subtle change in an air current across his bare chest.

continued

I could've stood holding
that skeleton-woman's hand a long time,
gazing on the suchness of her bones,
wondering who she'd been, how she
ended up in a university lab, knowing enough of the world
to surmise she'd died impoverished on the streets of some
desperate city, her bones fetching enough coins
                                        for a few relatives
to feed themselves through the period of mourning.

I turned back to my twenty-five students,
and we continued the class as the three
danced together in my imagination:
open-shirted Whitman,
                        my nameless ninth-grade partner, and
Sister Suzy Death with her wild, gap-toothed grin.

Lines from Nowhere

like trains out of a dark tunnel,
like fish rising to the sea's surface
on a moonless night in the dead of winter
in Antarctica, like leather wearing out
on comfortable shoes,
like a package of peas buried
in the corner of the freezer, gray-furred
green pellets of wayward nutrition, long
gone from the mother plant,
long ago harvested, shelled, and packaged,
sent into the world, in suspended
animation now, in deep organic sleep,
a hibernation of interrupted desire.
Thaw and cook them, let
them fulfill their vegetable desire
to transform into a human body,
food for words, which come
pouring onto the page, now,
Blake's energy of desire, the Kosmos
referring to itself and for itself,
game of games in which the seeker
is the sought.

II

Near

The Bird Incident

I dig this up even now with trepidation and shame though I have forgiven myself, the way an adult forgives a child, easily from that high plateau of maturity, that tableland above the urban chaos of the child's ferocious diminution and burning shame. The child still cannot climb to the cooling height. The adult has all the reasons and all the balm of explanations for the child's actions. And still a primal shame remains. The child squirms and wants to weep again just as he wept years ago

when he came upon a newly-hatched bird on the ground, at the foot of a high eucalyptus, the hatchling all pink and blue through skin as translucent as tissue paper, closed eyelids over swollen bulbs of blue ink, a few wing bristles as small and delicately stiff as the boy's mother's black mascara eyelash applicator, the only detail that lifts the hatchling out of the realm of absolute vulnerability – that and the limp prehistoric claws. On the tip of the bright yellow beak a chip of eggshell. The boy picks the bird up gently, weighs its small warmth in the palm of his hand, looks up at the straight tree trunk, as smooth, tall, and unassailable as a telephone pole. Is that a blackbird's nest in the unreachable branches? Where are the adult birds? There is only the silence of a tree at the edge of The Bush, a living but motionless hatchling, and a boy feeling the weight of a dilemma bearing down on him like a smothering dream. Desperately he wants to return the hatchling to its nest—though he has heard through the grapevine of children's lore that mother birds shove "defective" nestlings out, or worse, he suddenly remembers, once touched by human hands, wild things are not allowed back to nests or dens or burrows. Fallen, wingless, from such height, the baby bird is still, just the unmistakable warmth of its small life—ebbing. For the greater good—or the boy's eight-year old version of it—he struggles out from under the dilemma with the decision to euthanize the bird (not a word he knows). He carries it to a nearby pond, clear and still in the hot afternoon, staring undisturbed into the blue sky. He lowers the bird into the water. It sinks directly with just a few feeble strokes of its wing-nubs. It's what he feels as he acts that he remembers still — the pain in his chest, his own doubts: could the bird have lived if he'd taken it home, tried to feed it worms, kept it out of range of the cat?

What is still with me is the image of the bird gliding downward into the dark of the pond and a boy knee deep in water watching with an aching heart the consequences of his first real decision.

Nothing to Do, Nowhere to Go

after the TANG poets

At my feet, even the water spider
rests, unmoving on the still surface,
his eight feet dimpling the water's skin.

In the distance, on the other side,
a rowboat cradles a dozy fisherman.
The afternoon hums on the edge of sleep.

What should I be doing?
Surely work calls—chores, family?
The past is gone, the future

a dream of colors and light.
I'll take my cue from that duck
nestled on the embankment,

head tucked under wing,
one eye barely open, tilted up
at the hawk-empty sky.

Consulting the Akashic Record

for STEVE KOWIT,
after running me through a memory recovery process

I dive deep down
neural pathways, down
cultural, cross-generational
obscure tracks, deep
in earth memory
and re-call a scene
of one who was me
then in an ocean,
drowning,
an ancient ship in the distance
sinking, me sinking then shooting
straight up. . . .
nothing else, just
this fragment from the record
of one at the moment
of his death,
no emotion, no pain,
just pictures.
Memory and invention,
are they really separate?

Declarations and Promises

for KEN RICHARDSON

Friends, I'm giving up longing and yearning —
all dreams of heavens,
of archetypal returns to the deep
caves of the collective,
of a perfect love.
I for one, no longer seek salvation from
the benedictive kiss of the Divine Maiden.

Friends, you'll no longer smell
the cloying odor of hope around me,
just the body's unmistakable message,
blinking its millions of cells
into and out of existence.

Nor will you find me, Friends,
regretful or nostalgic.
Henceforth, I declare myself cured
of those two pernicious maladies!
And guilt — that bastard, useless emotion —
away with all its pointless suffering!

Friends, I promise you a new man.
I begin in earnest tomorrow!

Grace

descended in the night
like a nude down a staircase.

Was I that staircase
built of cell and bone?

Grace curved down through
DNA's spiraled helix,

and where she stepped
her naked foot lit up the spot.

Behind her trailed ecstasy
almost like an afterthought,

sheer as a negligee and lit
the dust, brushed it from each step.

I report this bliss as a witness,
it wasn't mine — just

as the way down the stairs
is not the stairs, though

they are a pair like the poem on
the page and the poem in the air.

Sideways, Down Rapids

He in the stern, she in the bow
desperately flailing and digging the paddles
thirty seconds of sheer terror
sliding by head-high boulders
covered by an inch-thick skin
of transparent water
and then the clear slow water
the calm drifting
the canoe capsizing now
for no good reason
the recriminations, the blaming,
the laughter.

Still Life:
Seven Keys on a Chain on a Table

Who would have thought it would come to this?
Seven keys to the kingdom that is my life,
seven talismen of hard brass and iron to open
five doors of four buildings,
one file cabinet, and one chariot of fire.

What a state of affairs for one
who started keyless
and will end keyless:
the boy who came home with empty pockets
to the only key in his life — if he even
needed that — under the mat,
dark, green-rimmed,
the door to that long-gone home,
in those days mostly open.

Tying Knots

The Boy Scout Manual was choked with them,
drawings of all the knots you'd ever need:
bowline, clove-hitch, cat's paw,
the elegant reef-knot—even its shadow,
the inept granny:

a knot to join splints over a broken leg or arm; a knot
to moor a boat or, with deft variation,
handcuff a criminal; a knot
to shorten a precious length of rope;
a knot to tie around someone's waist
and pull her up a cliff-face; a knot
for almost every emergency or trauma,
for any situation a prepared boy scout might encounter.

The drawings confused us.
Arrows and dotted lines tried to show
what to do with our two ends of rope.
We practiced for hours, trying to get them right.
Sometimes we experienced the grace of knots,
the difficult knot mastered,
like the magical sheepshank
whose purpose served,
would unravel with a roll of the wrist.

Sometimes we got into the real knots,
the nameless ones,
those lumpy, dispiriting knots
that led endlessly into themselves
like a no-exit French-existentialist question.

But mostly we learned
the legacy of sensible knots,
the ones there to serve us.
We learned patience, persistence;
we even learned that form followed function
(though we could never have said it).

We learned anything tied
could be untied, and anything untied
just left you back at the beginning — two ends
of one rope, your fingers itching.

The Piano Player
in the Hotel Lobby Bar

with a nod to WALLACE STEVENS

He has given himself
to one thing, to his own single art
and does not care for anything else, not
about the risk of lung cancer
from the cigarette between his lips, not
about the consequences of late nights
among strangers in this hotel bar, cares only
for what flows miraculously
after hours of sacrifice
through his fingers, sweet
jazz, timeless improvisations woven
from the warp and woof of the eternal
and shifting present,
plays with his entire being,
and nothing is important but the playing —
and the listening,
the playing that is the listening.

Something Vaguely Remembered

the memory of first snow
and the quality of its coldness
before coldness became a thing
to be avoided or resisted,

and along with that
the memory of sound, music specifically,
a child's xylophone, my own
or a playmate's, the crisp
icy clink of striking
the little metal bars,
the archetypal, Pythagorean,
almost divine
sound of notes,

as clear
as the memory of snow stuck playfully
down the back of my neck
and the beginning

of preference and choosing.

Madonna and Child

They'll never be the same for me again,
not since that art appreciation class
in the local museum, when the teacher
took us through the gallery and
we paused at a Renaissance painting,
and we really looked at it,
describing among ourselves
the foreground and background, the rich
brocaded cloth of the Madonna's gown, the crinkled
cotton of the child's white garment.
In the lower corner of the open window,
someone was plowing a field
and beyond him, the distant, bluing hills.
Then the teacher asked us if we noticed
anything about the mother and child,
and finally one of us observed
the child was looking away from the mother,
Jesus already looking past the world, his gaze
fixed on something distant, otherworldly.
Mary was looking to the side and down, modestly,
a little sad—not depressed, not a psychological state—
but pure dignified sadness, the human condition, her face
reflecting the knowledge that despite
grace, despite being the vehicle
for the birth of a god, life
is still sad, sad because you give birth
to a Christ who is also a human being,
who will suffer the pain
a mother can neither prevent nor tolerate.

Mother holding child, child in two worlds,
both of them on a holy mission from God,
the painter having succeeded at getting that down,
in her face the sheer humanity of the mother, her
sixteenth-century Italian teenaged beauty and innocence and
the wisdom of the ages and love, the little infant
with the big unwieldy body and
the expression already full of knowing and compassion
and just that little human edge, too,
of why me, Lord, why me?

When Pigs Fly

or, as in his dream in the pre-dawn of the fifth
day of the Zen retreat, when they glide . . . .

He's climbing a steep, ornate staircase
in some vast palatial building, the staircase narrowing
then abruptly ending.
He looks for the next flight of stairs, or
even a landing, is met with nothing
but a blank wall, much like the one
he's been facing these last days.
Panicked, he looks back down the staircase
as it zigs and zags, landing after landing,
disappearing into the fetid gloom below.
Gripped by fear and vertigo,
he looks again at the obdurate
white wall in front of him, when
a gift from the archetypal and not unhumorous
world of dreams, appears—a handle
and a bright, painted sign that says "Open!"
As he turns the handle, something begins to slide
out of the wall—a huge, pink, plastic pig,
looking like one of those old-time merry-go-round creatures.
The pig, too, sports little hand-holds
here and there on its surface with neatly
printed signs, "Grab me" and "Hang on tight."
He mounts the pig,
now warm and alive and soft,
a sow; he's certain because he whispers
into the soft bristles of her ear, something
like, "What now?" or "Where to next?"
He spurs her gently with his bare heels
and she moves slowly away from the wall,
begins to glide in a long, shallow spiral
downward.
From far below music floats up,
something stately and baroque at first
that changes into a soulful folksong
as they float down.

Somehow, he feels elated and safe, grateful
as he continues to ride the pig down.
Now, the floor of the voluminous atrium
changes into a vast plain seen
below indistinctly through skeins of mist.
Still they spiral down, the dreamer
and his dream pig, until the ground
finally appears clearly.
With one more graceful quarter arc,
the pig lands with a squishing slide just
as the morning sun slants in and lights up
the familiar pig-pen world
with its rollicking and terrible life,
its incandescent pearly mud.

A Philosophy of Life

At the dinner party, Contessa, our hostess,
a lovely woman, though with a reputation
for not putting up with anyone's guff, bluntly
asked our friend Ike to cut to the chase and confess
his "philosophy of life" — mind you, right then
and there among the mushroom pate
                              and roasted artichoke hearts —
that she didn't have time for niceties or
                              beating around the bush, life was
too short, etc., all this after one of Ike's characteristically
misanthropic comments on human beings — he likes
to refer to us as *homo satanicus*, what with our long
history of wars, slavery, cruelty.
To his great credit, Ike took the question seriously,
paused, drew a deep breath, and simply declared himself
a skeptical mystic
or maybe it was a mystical skeptic.

Oddly, or not, this seemed to satisfy our hostess,
Ike not having much of a chance to elaborate beyond
referring to those moments we've all had
when everything pauses, or comes together, when all
is seen as connected, non-dual, miraculous, luminous —
whatever your favorite way of putting it.

At that moment, I deeply admired my friend Ike.
Indeed, what other "philosophy of life "
                              could possibly hold up
in this paradoxical and heart-breaking world, this world
of leukemia and lollipops, catnip and catastrophe,
Abu Ghraib and avocados? The skeptic says,
                              "I can't fully believe
anything you tell me because, really, how
the bloody hell do you know?"
And the mystic says, "Yes, like Rumi's, Dogen's, Teresa's,
and a host of others', my own experience is all
I can finally rely on, even though
I might be completely mistaken."

So, when the sun rises over the mountain
and the valley awakens with the mockingbird's
call and the coyote's (or wolf's, or dingo's, or hyena's)
last perplexed yip at the vanishing moon,
or when the walls collapse and we fall into
the bottomless black hole of
Stillness and Silence, what else, returning,
is there to say but yes, and yes again.
But, please, don't take my word for it.

There's What You Do

and then there's what you feel
while you do it
and then there're the words
that come later
to describe, recreate, narrate it —
all at a third remove
from the doing. And
then there's poetry,
a doing in words, the act of writing
and a pointing back to
the ultimate and absolute
through the relativity of words,
their limited and limiting circumscriptions,
their stalactites of feeling,
their penumbras of meaning,
the deep cave of their origins.

Toes

ten blind mice
two platoons on night patrol

five sets of mirrored
partners dimly seen

two crews sailing
changing leads back and forth

revolutionaries
trapped in dark cells

a monastic order
of lonesome monks

Of

Humble little word, pointing to others,
obscure, in the shadows cast by
important nouns, unobtrusive, shy servant
in the impossible position of serving
two masters, one always coming, one
always going.
"OF," of thee I sing,
where would we be without you,
little verbal gluer, relationship maker?
Sprinkled throughout our texts, our speeches,
our days, you bind the words together,
the names, the references, the self-important pronouns,
the ubiquitous I and me, mine, my — for love of
me, for love of God and
money . . . . No rest for you, little humble servant, of
all the words, you are of
the utmost importance, you
and your ragamuffin cousins, spread
throughout our sentences
rarely together in one place.
This poem shall bring you together,
we will have a party of
prepositions, conjunctions, connectives . . . .
Like true science and our own precious experience,
you show us ultimately there's nothing
but relationship, our very nouns carryovers
from earlier, perhaps, simpler times.
You give the lie to our arrogant assurance,
our belief that all the parts
could be counted and named, divided and sub-
divided down to one nameable thing, a
building block, a some *thing* on
which to rest . . . .
So, here in this poem, you are.

Let's throw a party, a relational party, a
the self-important stink of
pronouns, without
the endless parade of
nouns flexing their pumped-up
torsos, without those flashy verbs, neurotic in
their endless activity . . . .
Oh, and let's not invite those
popinjay adjectives and
adverbs, the hood ornaments of language, what
a relief to be away
from their glints and flashes in
the noonday sun . . . .
No more those huge, abstract nouns that
roll in like dense fog or
the invading tanks of a dreaded army, blanketing or
crushing all in their path:
freedom, boredom, hope, nobility, glory . . . and
those little specific nouns, seemingly modest but
also ultimately vain, with one eye always cocked at
the mirror, proud of
their gem-like specificity:
mote, follicle, rain,
carcinoma, communiqué, opal, etc.
Come, my little friends, choose up partners for
the dance: *of with and, but with though, under with for,*
so with to, with with when . . . .
Or gather in groups, gesturing silently, raising an
eyebrow here, nodding there, a
subtle wink, a shift of
the body: *on under by yet,*
from though since for when,
nor because as if . . . .

continued

Better still, dance the circle dance, join
hands, fall together in an
orgiastic heap, show those
nouns and pronouns what
the world is truly, sing, together at
last all that is relational, that
brings all together, the already-
but-unseen-togetherness,
the ultimate unified field theory in
action right here in this poem as
everywhere/nowhere else, not
string but the absence of string, the
zero at the heart of any metaphor, the
absence of everything, therefore the presence of
All which is the presence of
No thing, just
the presence of
presence.

Knuckles

mountain range to the east
mountain range to the west
the body in the world
the world in the body

One More Attempt
at Self-Definition

I come from a tribe
of nature worshippers.
Pantheists, believers in fairies,
forest sprites, and wood nymphs,
who heard devils in their windmills,
met them in the woods, cloven-hooved
and dapper gentlemen of the night,
who named the god of thunder,
who praised and glorified bread,
dark rye waving
waist-high out of earth,
and held it sacred, who spent afternoons
mushrooming in forests
of pine, fir, and birch,
who transferred Jesus
from his wooden cross,
transformed Him
into a wood-carved, worrying peasant,
raised Him on a wooden pole above the crossroads
where He sat with infinite patience
in rain and snow, wooden legs apart,
wooden elbows on wooden knees,
wooden chin in wooden hand,
worrying and sorrowing for the world . . .
these people who named their sons and daughters
after amber, rue, dawn, storm,
and the only people I know who have a diminutive
form for God Himself — *Dievulis*, "God-my-little-buddy."

No wonder I catch myself speaking
to trees, flowers — these eucalyptus, so far
from Eastern Europe — or that I bend down to the earth,
gather pebbles, acorns, leaves, boles, bring
them home, enshrine them on mantelpieces
or above porcelain fixtures, any wonder
I grow nervous in rooms
and must step outside and touch a tree,
or sink my toes in dirt, watch the birds fly.

My Life Is Over

My life, I mean that life
defined by narrow boundaries,
concerns, by survival
and whining and looking over
my shoulder, that life
of the bag of skin
and bones with the little
fascist ego bitching
and strutting all day long.
Happy to say that little Mussolini
is dead. Well, if not
dead — stripped
of his shiny black uniform,
insignia cut off pockets and collars,
epaulettes popped
off shoulders.
Not yet fully naked
but on the way, down
to T, shorts, socks.

Whistling Woman

What new woman is this?
What twenty-first century
phenomen-*a*!?
Bopping along,
her thick-heeled boots
whomp the pavement,
snug peddle-pushers,
exposed midriff, silver stud
in her outie belly button.

What complex and virtuoso
trills and whistle-yodels,
what inter-melodic
jazz riffs and glissandos!

This confident, extroverted
young female striding
the postmodern urban landscape —
she picked the right
new century to whistle
the world's attention
onto herself.

Stopping into a Church:
North Beach

for FEDERICO MORAMARCO

After Sunday morning croissants and cappuccinos
in the famous Cafe Trieste among the slouch-hatted literatti,
and after gazing into the window-displayed books
of not-yet-opened City Lights, we set off down the street
for an innocent stroll in *the city everyone loves*.

We pass the cafes, avant-garde art galleries,
Italian restaurants, and come
to a large church and an open park.
It's the Church of St. Peter and Paul —
St. Peter *and* St. Paul, mind you,
both of them, the two big guns
of the Catholic Church, the one the rock, the other
the eternal voice of restraint and sin.

And I see the church is run by the Salesians,
and I'm back in Crystal Lake, Indiana, pimply-faced,
fifteen years old, my first year in this country,
my first real job: boy's summer camp kitchen-helper,
grass-cutter, and for the first time, altar boy.

We climb the stone stairs, push open the huge doors, step in.
Of course — and I've forgotten this — it's Mass,
the priest intoning away in English
                         (not the fond Latin of my youth),
years since I've been to Mass.
We stand in the back, just inside the door —
                                  awkwardly, I think,
and yet at home in a way, too: there's nothing quite like
a huge Catholic church, and this one
                         approaches a cathedral, really —
cherubim floating, the stained
glass windows with their inky blues, crimsons,
                                  divine purples,

the colored light slanting through in epiphinal shafts
through myriad motes of dust
onto the parishioners at floor level,
the men all hatless, the women, heads covered.

I'm surprised — even amazed — at how many people are here.
After all, this is San Francisco, North Beach, birth place
of the Beats, the center of hippiedom, *the City by the Bay*,
                                        but here they all are,
and here are Fred and I,
two long-time lapsed Catholics, dropping in
on old Mother Church.
One of us almost crosses himself on the way out,
the other one does.

An Evening Walk in Assisi

After dinner, I walk out of the Hotel Giotto, up
the winding street. Elsewhere, this would be called
                                        the gloaming,
the air sweet and darkening, the distant Umbrian hills
fading into mist.

From both sides of the narrow street,
                              the medieval houses lean
toward each other like old friends hunched
over a chessboard. Countless swallows swoop and dive,
play at the edge of night
before settling down under eaves.

I walk up the cobbled street, past open
windows and doors spilling the smells of Mama's dinner,
voices of TVs and radios, rock 'n' roll.
In my modest pilgrimage — that's what it's becoming —
                                        I know

continuing will bring me to the piazza at the top of the hill
and the church we visited earlier.
But I've been to enough churches today.

I'm content with this little winding street,
how it goes up and up like a vine,
through all the clinging life,
and how, in the deepening dark,
I turn and come back down.

The Moon above the Map

Looking at maps as a child,
I imagined I was high in the air
above the world.
If I brought my face
down closer to the paper
I believed I would see the fields
and the cities opening up
their secrets to me.
I tried to focus my eyes
microscopically
down into the textured paper.
It was only a matter of getting near enough.

In the Background

It happened again, today:
I looked up and found myself in the corner
of a tourist's camera lens, another
piece of my soul caught momentarily,
hung in the background like a painting within
a painting, a little blurred, indistinct,
the shadow of something important,
to be carried back to — this time — Japan
and pored over by the family
reviewing their visit to America:
there's Koji, sunglasses and all, next to Akiko
all her doubts hidden behind a fixed expression.
Perhaps by now, as the family of voyeurs
gobble up the images, Akiko and Koji
have worked it all out. How could they have not,
what with seagulls and battleships
and that small figure in the background
like an angel on their shoulder.

A Reading on the Milosz Steps

Vilnius, October, 2011

for CZESLAW MILOSZ (1911- 2004)

I took my turn in American-accented English,
  read out loud your memorable "Blacksmith Shop"
  with its startling final line of the poet's calling —
your calling — "to glorify things just because they are."

    Czeslaw, you might've enjoyed this odd occasion,
  a score of your fellow poets gathered together
  by fate like a small tribe, some smoking, huddling
to stay warm, if not by bellows' blaze by word glow on a cold

    autumn afternoon in the baroque city of your youth.
  From your distant boyhood came the heat of the blacksmith's
  shop, the clang of iron, the barefoot boy in the open doorway
backlit by a green meadow, years ago, gazing on in wonder . . . .

    In an hour we honored you — you'd be embarrassed
  if I said "glorified" — by reading your poems in all our
  languages, right there on the mystery of steps that simply
are but go both up and down just because we say they do,

    and we celebrated the gift your life was to us all,
  in the end, just because it had been and, through
  all those years and decades of poems, of careful words,
of the poet's attention to what was in front of you, still is.

107

Watching a Day

go by, entirely focused
on its seamless presence,
that square of
sunlight inching across
the tile floor
and that carpet with its secret
hieroglyphics and
unreadable meanings.

Sitting and watching, walking
and watching, listening
to birds and coyotes and bells
and the hum
of your own aliveness.

From dawn to dusk
to deep night
being just this,
just this.

Zen retreat, October-November, 2010

The Cross-Court Top-Spin
Backhand Passing Shot

for STEPHEN DUNN

It still lives perfectly among all failures
and disappointments, among frustrations

of games played with long-lost friends
on courts now sprouting trees, in nightmares

where balls explode in a puff of dust
on the put-away volley.

At odd moments it comes back, an instant
replay, saved forever:

walking down a supermarket aisle
or crossing a parking lot alone at night,

my shoulder drops knees bend arm cocks
stepforward stroke elbowlocked wristrolls slightly

followthrough salute
my opponent lunging balldipping fast under

his flailing racquet and hitting sweetly
on the outside edge of base and sideline's T.

For every one of those perfect shots
a hundred curses, stumbles, faults,

unforced errors, scores of white or yellow balls
that have sailed out of the court

over the wire fence last seen bright
and round against the azure sky of youth.

A Stillborn Son Speaks

Had I lived, forward into that life
I never knew, back
I could look, back and recall
this timeless, seamless present, this now
where history furls out its petals,
releases its brief aroma, curls, and falls into dust.

And like you, the living,
I could inspect each mote, indulge
the nostalgic itch for wasting now
for then to make that then glow . . . .

But I was a mere coalescence
of failed potentialities, just a voice to say
whatever you say about what happened
is what happened,
though that's not it at all.

Dressing Down

The dark blue suit,
the snappy corduroy jacket
with its English Prof
leather elbow patches
hang now in the guest room closet
attracting silverfish.

Two pricey silk neckties — the remaining
best of the lot — drape forlornly over
a hanger. They're unlikely to
fly in the breeze or
strangle much anymore.

My academic gown and its puffy
medieval cap, worn once a year
these last forty-four,
have been dropped off
at the local Good Will.

Two pairs of dress shoes,
one black, one cordovan,
lie in their plastic boxes high on
the columbarium of shelves
in the dusty garage.

In shorts, T-shirt, sandals,
on an incomparable
Southern California weekday morning,
I raise a mug of coffee, a grateful toast
to this new life,
to what's in front of me,
this almost empty parking lot,
this scrap of paper.

Unreliable Narrators

to my literary colleagues, and to BILL SULLIVAN

As professors of literature, we loved
to split hairs over
the intricacies of point of view,
angle of narration, whether
narrators were to be trusted or not,
whether they were alter-egos of The Author
(if such an Old God existed anymore,
we took delight in saying)
and other such fascinating formal
questions — all of which, I now realize, were rather
clever evasions of a more honest response to
Literature, something like,
"Well, dang, how 'bout that *Moby Dick*?!"

I'm retired now, withdrawn
from the rodeo of Academia, spurs
no longer a-jangle on my desert boots,
so I can indulge a certain flippancy about
these formerly vital questions. But really,
what narrator can ever be truly reliable?
Seeing my old friend Bill recently, it became
disturbingly clear his memory
of an event differs entirely from mine:

As I recall — mind you, this over
forty years ago in grad school —
we were hiking through the woods
somewhere near Devil's Slide along the Weber River.
We came across a young doe
who had hung herself up on a barbed wire fence,
probably in exuberant mid leap.
How long she'd been there,
we couldn't tell — she still had a wild, alert eye.

We approached carefully —
she started to panic, tufts of fur
twanged on the barbs — but I
managed to grab her back legs,
lifted and hoisted them over the wire strand, and
she bounded off as gracefully as, well,
as a gazelle happy to be free again, and
none the worse for wear.

Given my theme, you may guess
Bill remembers this incident
completely differently
as having taken place not with me your
Humble Narrator but with his son —
in an entirely different time and place!
He, too, has written a poem about it.

Dear Reader, I can't swear to my story, though
I love it dearly, and neither, I suppose,
can Bill swear to his (I could tell he was unsettled
at the possibility his memory had holes in it
as I am about mine).
So here am I, your self-confessed
Unreliable Narrator, a kind of literary trope
within my own life-story, and I can only
bow in apology for the limitations of
my selective and self-serving memory,
though glad for the moment to
be outside of all those stories and theories
we create and then believe in
whole-heartedly, passionately,
as if they were the dear Lord's own irrefutable Truth.

Outside the Café, Late Morning

In the half-empty parking lot,
a crow and a seagull
argue over some discards:

Crow, on the pavement, tries to pry
up a dried, flattened piece of fast food.
Seagull, all white and grey, yellow-eyed,
rides the air just above him, flutters expertly,
squawks and carries on.

If I must take sides, I go with Crow — after all,
Seagull's a good ten miles from the coast.
Seagull concedes Crow's
claim, arcs up and off with a few wing beats,
a final plaintive cry, and
heads due west.

Crow finally succeeds
with his food and paper mess
and hauls it up to the overhanging branch
of a nearby eucalyptus.

The parking lot returns to
its dour and stained functionality.
My fellow humans ease in and out of their vehicles,
self-absorbed, a little puffed up,
lost under the autumn sky.

114

Not Really Lucid Dreaming

It seems I'm delayed on my journey home. What was to be a short trip, a mere domestic errand, finds me in Sydney, Australia picking up my car outside a suburban train station like the ones of my youth — is it Bankstown, or Yagoona, or Regents Park?

I remind myself to drive on the left side and speed off in my spanking new 1953 Holden FJ sedan. Now, I'm dialing my wife on the cell to tell her I may be a little late. After all, I'm in Sydney (and she's in San Diego). The connection's not the best, but I hear myself saying, "Honey, I'll be a little late, but I want you to know that I know this is a dream, so please don't worry. If I'm late, it's just because this is a dream."

All this I'm saying, one hand on the cell, one on the wheel, looking into the rearview mirror as the car speeds backwards.

Seen at the Mall

The plump teenybopper,
dark shiny hair bouncing
on her shoulders, sweet-faced
and vulnerable despite
surface Attitude applied
like inexpert makeup,
trails a step behind
her look-a-like though
heavier, tougher mother.

In her innocence, has the girl
already bought into
love-as-commodity, herself as
precious love object, shelf-life limited?
Does she really believe
her own mauve T-shirt with its dark
pink heart split open by
one of those cartoon lightning bolts,
the two halves still pinned across the gap
by Cupid's arrow, blood-red letters
above and below,

You break it
You buy it?

A Recent Retiree from Academia Rejoices at Not Being Interviewed by the Accrediting Team

Today, I am being interviewed
by Sun and her dear friend Shade—
Are you warm, are you cool, they ask?
Yes, I am. Thank you so much.
Good, they say, we hope to be back for
our scheduled follow-up visits tomorrow
and tomorrow. If you see him tonight,
say hi to Moon.

Dreaded Doppelgängers

The Java Joint has just changed hands,
the new owner, a recently retired cop.
Along with all of us regulars,
his buddies still on the Force
now make it their daily pit stop.

So this morning I confess
a slight dismay at all this sudden Authority
around me, that subtle threat of violence
in the squad cars and motorcycles nuzzling
the curb, those deadly black side-arms
holstered and slung low
like Hollywood gunslingers,
the mirrored sunglasses in which I see only
my transgressing and diminished self.

O.K., I'll try for a little more compassion,
try to remember our Friends in Uniform
behind their badges are likely just
as fearful as the rest of us,
and they too crave their morning caffeine fixes.

Surely, each one of us has a place in this life,
a moving point along the spiral
of whatever growth we can tie ourselves to.
And we'll always need the police,
won't we, to catch the thieves, the meth dealers,
the rapists and murderers.

Patrolmen, Sergeants, Detectives, Inspectors,
Men and Women in Blue, America's Finest —
Dear Peace Officers, may you all
enjoy some peace of mind just for now on
this bright start of day, as
you consume your mild drug of choice
(dare I, from a nearby table, toast you with my double latté?)

before you have to Code 3 it out of here,
sirens ablare, red and blue lights flashing,
to keep us safe from our dreaded doppelgängers,
those who actually do
what most of us only imagine we could do.

The Bridge of Eternal Love

at the Republic of UŽUPIS

is small and modest, traversed
in a dozen strides
spanning a narrow
fast-flowing river in a recently reclaimed
small part of Europe
surrounded by a crumbling bohemian old town
near a few baroque churches so
ordinary and out of place
they might remind you
of a brood of red and amber chickens
dust-bathing and dozing
on hillocks of dirt in the afternoon sun
somewhere back in your childhood,
if your childhood were in the 17th century.

On that riverbank, there's a tavern
with an outdoor patio and benches and
chairs and small tables
for lovers or friends,
too cold to sit at today
though inside the poets have gathered
for a festive reading and hearing
of each others' verses, and
of course, for some drinking.

The Bridge of Eternal Love —
let's just name it that — because
after all, it bristles with scores of padlocks
some shiny, some rusted,
each locked onto an iron rail or
a metal pillar, or even onto another padlock,
each padlock clamped
to the bridge by hopeful lovers and newlyweds
who have tossed their keys
into the waters below

under the cool and objective
gaze of the bare-breasted mermaid who sits on
her fused and unspreadable fishtail-legs
on the threshold of her alcove above the river.

Oh, lovers, may you always return
to your bridge to celebrate the long life
of your love, to admire
and show off your very own padlock
as it weathers the seasons,
your initials, the heart and arrow
deeply engraved, and not
return, in dead of night (one of you)
through the moonshadows of those churches,
extra key or hacksaw in hand
to unlock or saw off
your ex-lover's and your padlock
and drop it sadly into the flowing
waters to rest on the bottom,
ignominious among all
those true eternal lovers' keys.

Have You Ever Noticed

late at night
turning over in your bed
the body restless, sleepless,
in the grip of jittery insomnia,
that even as it jumps from
side to side
like a grasshopper from
one blade to another,
the field doesn't move at all, is
utterly still and silent.
Now, if I were Kabir, I might say,
"Kabir says, 'Who needs sleep then?'"

Trakai Castle

Come with me to a certain medieval castle,
a short day's horseback ride from
the city with three names: Vilnius, Wilno, Vilna—
depending on your preferred conqueror.
With our hundred horses, we'll drive it in an hour.
Follow me to one of the castle's vaulted-ceiling rooms,
and please note those two odd-looking chairs and small table.
See how they're huddled in their threesomely intimacy,
as cozy a little menage à trois of domestic furniture
as any you'd see in a modern kitchenette.
It's hard for me to say what you'll notice first, whether
the furniture's intimacy, its style, or form, the sheer facts
of its material composition, its Platonic
ur-chair-ness manifesting from the realm of universal forms.
But surely, by now, whatever your metaphysical orientation,
you've noticed—yes,
                    I can see the look of shock on your face—
that our little intimate dinette is made of animal parts:
the legs of the chairs are not metaphorical but
the taxonomically redone real legs
of some centuries-dead ox or elk,
                         the cloven hooves splayed out
at the unnatural angle of a ballet dancer's plié.
See, too, how the armrests are made of smooth ox horns,
the back rests from interlocking deer and elk antlers.
Yes, you're right, the table is supported by more antlers,
the tabletop itself a sliced section of oak tree
and on it, two horn goblets for drinking mead.
Let's also note the animal hides covering the seats
and the bearskin rug spread out before it all.

Have you been to the Ripley's Believe It Or Not Museum
in St. Augustine, Florida?
Have you seen the vest knitted from human hair,
the little jewelry box made from fingernail clippings?
Ancient medieval castle,
            20th century pop-culture museum, home—
as always, the horrific, the fascinating, the domestic
inseparably on display together.

123

My Mother's Thumbs

In her last years, my mother
suffered from painfully cracked thumbs
that no amount of doctoring or
treatment could cure.

We all tried to help her, researching
salves and ointments,
internal supplements,
gloves and moist heat,
some of us even resorting to
metaphysical solutions
(thumbs represent peace of mind)
but to no avail.
The condition persisted to her
dying day. I know because we held
her hand, my sister and I,
that long Christmas Eve,
its bird-like fragile warmth
which gripped firmly early on
then only rested unmoving
until it never moved again
and death had cured all her ills.

And now I sometimes find my own
thumbs cracked and painful,
unresponsive to treatment, but
strangely welcoming this
as a remembrance of my mother,
who would ask, towards the end
in her dementia of forgetting
only one thing, to please
please not forget her.

The Pearl of Great Price

What is it,
this pearl of great price?
this thing made from accident and irritation?
the grit that floats in
and lodges under the tender flesh
and can't be thrown out, will not
go away and so must be taken in
and worked on and worked with,
made of the very minerals and juices of the body,
the accretions of worry and suffering,
rounded off and smoothed finally,
seen as a gift at last to ourselves
and therefore to the world.

A Flaneur

If he could do it all again,
he'd be one of those young, monied
gentilhommes of Paris
during the *Belle Epoque*
in the last half of the 19th century . . . .

He'd step out his door
look *droit et gauche*, aim himself
down the *Rue de Quelque Chose*
with the confidence and open heart
of youth, daily hatched anew as an artist.
Oh, he'd be a blue flame, trembling
with potential and possibility . . . .

Down the gorgeously woven carpet
of his youthful destiny
he'd glide lightly, buoyantly, follow
it across the square, *le parc*,
past the shops and cafes, follow
the unrolling poem of his life,
alert to the nameless something
that can't be caught or expressed but
must be, nonetheless,
what Art's for . . . .
Our flaneur would saunter along
the inclination of the moment
through city streets, the labyrinth
of his own dreams, his daemon
whispering in his ear all the way . . . .

At a haberdasher's on the *Place Pas de Quoi*
he'd pause to look at the fashionable
new *chapeaux*, note his reflection in the *fenêtre*,
(thank *Dieu* for high school French!) bend
a little to situate himself under
one of the hats, laugh, catch
a glimpse of the parasoled *mademoiselle's*
reflection behind him in the 19th century glass
of that Parisian shop window
on a bright spring morning
with nothing to do but gather
material for a poem or a painting
and follow his heart
where it would lead that day.

The Cat

The cat sits perfectly
as only cats can,
with clouds and wind,
with the moon,
with ancient Egypt,
with All That Is.
Tail wrapped classically around
front paws, ears pivoting
independently, monitoring
those certain sounds,
eyes half-closed and turned
inward
distantly,
aware nonetheless
of the outside world:
the subtle changes in shade and light,
the arrival and departure of birds,
a lizard
sunning on the fence —
this amazing cat
simply sitting
on an easy chair
on a patio,
this inexplicable being
who has never once written out
a check for anything,
never driven
a car, never once
made a false move,
never read
nor uttered
a single word.

An Old Story

Across from the house
where I grew up
lived an old couple
whose shadows slowly
passed behind windows
as we children
played in the street
crying out in our joy and wonder.

And here I am now
half of an old couple
behind winter windows listening
to children play in our cul de sac
as a dark sky
deepens and settles
and I swear I can hear
my own voice
calling out in the street.

Emily Dickinson's Envelopes

Besides neatly stitched fascicles,
bundled and saved for
presumed posterity,
Emily practiced a frugal husbandry
where paper was concerned, penciled
poems on envelopes unhinged
and splayed out from their folded forms.
She built her own lines to conform
to their triangular flaps and rectangles
as if the secret of envelopes —
those carriers of love and anguish —
told her all she needed to know
in this world about containment
and revelation.

Chips

You and I
We
are All
chips off
the Old Block,
the Old Block, black
Silent and Empty
and Unutterably Still

Twice Dead

Once, long ago, reaching for
a jar of peanut butter
from the refrigerator, I saw
a fly dead on the lid, actually
dead on his feet—all six of them.
His blue-green thorax
reminded me then of a cheap tuxedo
or the shiny vest of a waiter.

Had the fly died of cold, I wondered?
Had he been poisoned by a smear of peanut butter?
Could he have died of fly old age?
It was way beyond me . . . but, surely, to die
on your feet and remain standing,
that was something!

When I brought the jar closer to my eye,
a small kitchen breeze
nudged the fly off his death perch, and he fell
somersaulting once or twice
and landed on the floor—
again, dead on his feet!

But wait, was he really dead?
Just to be sure, I got down
and blew on him gently
and he skated along the linoleum.
He did not flip over.

I blew once more and he slid
into a dust ball, and was truly held,
though not for long, no bug in amber, he.
Flightless dead fly, insignificant—
neither comedy, tragedy, nor melodrama—
why has your tiny post-mortem story
stayed with me—and re-surfaced
all these years later?

All the Advice I Need
I Find in Songs

Get back to where you belong
cause the thrill is gone
and ain't nobody home
and there ain't no cure for love

get yourself a green and yellow basket
forget your perfect offering
what did the deep sea say?
Who stole the keeshka?
By a lonely prison wall
I heard a young girl calling

Do you mind if I sit down here by your graveside?
Help me, Rhonda!
I waltzed my Matilda all over.
But when Quinn the Eskimo gets here . . . .
Oh yes, oh yes, my love, I'll get you
Most anything

Morning has broken like the first morning
I would swim over the deepest ocean.

ABOUT THE POET

B orn in Austria of Lithuanian parents, AL ZOLYNAS grew up in Sydney, Australia and Chicago. He lived in Salt Lake City, in Marshall and St. Paul, Minnesota, and in San Diego. At various times, he has been a kitchen helper, lifeguard, worker in a felt factory, cab driver, road construction worker, poetry editor, resident poet in the schools, Minnesota Out Loud Traveling Poet, volunteer for the Hunger Project, and Fulbright-Hays Fellow to India. He holds academic degrees from the University of Illinois (B.A.) and the University of Utah (M.A. and PhD.).

For 42 years, he taught literature and writing at universities in Utah, Minnesota, and California. His poems have been widely printed in magazines and anthologies, and he is the author of three books of poems: *The New Physics,* Wesleyan University Press: 1979; *Under Ideal Conditions,* Laterthanever Press: 1994 (San Diego Book Award, Best Poetry); and *The Same Air.* Intercultural Studies Forum: 1997.

Al's poems have been translated into Lithuanian, Spanish, Ukrainian, and Polish — the last by Nobel Laureate CZESLAW MILOSZ. Six of his poems are featured in the movie, *Fighting Words* (Indican Pictures, Los Angeles). With FRED MORAMARCO, he co-edited *Men of Our Time: An Anthology of Male Poetry in Contemporary America,* 1992, and *The Poetry of Men's Lives: An International Anthology* (San Diego Book Award for Best Poetry Anthology: 2005), both from the University of Georgia Press.

He has completed translating (from Lithuanian) the memoir, *The Parallels of Dita: Surviving Nazism and Communism in Lithuania,* by Silvija Lomsargytė-Pukienė.

Retired from Alliant International University in San Diego, he currently practices and teaches meditation in Escondido, California, where he lives with his wife and their cat.

Acnowledgements

Grateful acknowledgment is made to the following books, journals, magazines, and anthologies in which some of these poems have appeared:

Australian Poetry: The Finest Recent Australian Poetry
Big Toe Review
Break Out of the Box
Burning With a Vision: Poetry of Science and the Fantastic
Cafe Solo
California Quarterly
Canard Anthology
City Works
Cordite Poetry Review, No. 6 and 7, Sydney, Australia
Druskininkai Poetry Anthology
Editor's Choice III: Fiction, Poetry, & Art from the U.S. Small Press
Hunger and Thirst: Food Literature
Lasting: Poems on Aging
Lithuania: In Her Own Words:
        an Anthology of Contemporary Lithuanian Writing
Lituanus, Volume 49, Number 2
The Maverick Poets Anthology
A New Geography of Poets
The New Zoo Review , Vol. 1, Richmond, VA (Sunken Meadow Press)
The No-Street Poet's Voice
*Nueva Poesia de Los Angeles (*University of Guadalajara, Mexico)
Plain Song
Poem Hunter
Poetry International, 2, San Diego State University
The Poetry of Men's Lives: An International Anthology
            (University of Georgia Press, Athens and London)
Poly: New Speculative Poetry
Portfolio
Pushing the Envelope: Epistolary Poems
Quadrant
San Diego Poetry Annual
San Diego Writers' Monthly
Stand Up Poetry Anthology
Technology in American Literature
Trees Project (forthcoming)
Tsunami
The Umbral Anthology
Velocities: A Magazine of Speculative Poetry
The Wallace Stevens Journal
Writing on the Edge

135

CREDITS

COVER AND FRONTISPIECE:
The Great Three-Fingered Nebula
photograph by BOB INGRAHAM

POET (BACK COVER): *Holding Elrond*
photograph by JULIANA ZOLYNAS

I: FAR (PAGE 3): *Light Years*
Illustration by RILEY PRATO

II: NEAR (PAGE 73): *Entering Atmosphere*
Illustration by RILEY PRATO

POET (PAGE 135): *Writing, with Nelson*
photograph by ARLIE ZOLYNAS

BY THE SAME AUTHOR

The New Physics
Wesleyan University Press: 1979

Under Ideal Conditions
Laterthanever Press: 1994
San Diego Book Award: Best Poetry

The Same Air
Intercultural Studies Forum: 1997

•

Co-Editor, with FRED MORAMARCO

Men of Our Time:
An Anthology of Male Poetry in Contemporary America
University of Georgia Press: 1992

The Poetry of Men's Lives: An International Anthology
University of Georgia Press: 2005
San Diego Book Award: Best Poetry Anthology

•

TRANSLATION

The Parallels of Dita:
Surviving Nazism and Communism in Lithuania
by SILVIJA LOMSARGYTĖ-PUKIENĖ
Jotema Press of Vilnius: 2004
Lymer & Hart (forthcoming: 2020)

137

Made in the USA
Lexington, KY
23 November 2019